TUDOR HALL:
THE BOISSEAU FAMILY FARM

Arthur W. Bergeron, Jr.

ISBN: 0-87517-099-4

Printed by
The Dietz Press
Richmond, Virginia

TABLE OF CONTENTS

ILLUSTRATIONS

INTRODUCTION

Prior to 1861, Tudor Hall was a successful farm. It was an example of the level of prosperity many Southerners hoped to reach. Tudor Hall typified the system of land and labor found across the region. The farm produced cash crops on large landholdings by using slave labor. The Boisseau family, which owned and operated the farm, were energetic business people. By investing and managing well, they made Tudor Hall profitable. Tudor Hall began as a tobacco farm, growing the cash crop most typical of antebellum Virginia. Tobacco exhausted the soil, so in time the Boisseaus began diversifying the crops they grew. They adopted new agricultural practices and took advantage of new farm tools and machinery. Thus, the Boisseaus were able to maintain their comfortable lifestyle while some other Virginians did not.

The Civil War altered the lives of millions of ordinary Americans, including the Boisseaus. Events on and near the farm in 1864-1865 abruptly changed Tudor Hall forever, destroying the prosperous lifestyle its owners had known. As a result of the war, the system of land and labor collapsed across the South. Land values fell and personal wealth declined dramatically. The slaves were free, and many planters and farmers could no longer produce cash crops on their land. The landscapes of many farms were destroyed by earthworks and rifle pits. Trees had been cut, and outbuildings and fences ripped down. Fields were a sea of dust or mud, depending upon the weather. Many farm animals had disappeared for use by the armies or for food. The story of Tudor Hall and the Boisseau family helps us to explore and understand how that drama unfolded.

CHAPTER 1

THE BOISSEAUS
BUILD TUDOR HALL

The story of Tudor Hall begins with the acquisition by William E. Boisseau of 100 acres in Dinwiddie County in 1810. William was the descendant of a French Huguenot family that had arrived in the county during the 1730s. The Huguenots, who were Protestants, had fled France in the late 1600s, and many of them had gone to England before migrating to America. Two brothers, Joseph E. and James, arrived in the New World about 1689. James settled in Virginia. Either he or his son purchased land in Dinwiddie County in 1739. James Boisseau's property was along Hatcher's Run and Gravelly Run, two streams south of the parcel acquired by William. It is believed that William's father was Benjamin Boisseau and that William's land had originally been part of his father's holdings. Tax records for 1800 show a William Boisseau, described as "over 16," living with a Benjamin Boisseau. The family was taxed for six horses, ten slaves, and a carriage described as a "2-wheel chair."

Dinwiddie County had been created from Prince George County by an act of the Virginia General Assembly in 1752. Farmers from the Tidewater area of the state had begun moving into Dinwiddie to take advantage of the thousands of acres of fertile land found there. These farmers were slave owners and planted their property in the main cash crop of the day--tobacco. Boisseau's status in the county as a tobacco farmer was such that by 1820 he had received an appointment as a tobacco inspector in Petersburg. The town of Petersburg, which had been incorporated in 1784, became the port through which the tobacco was shipped to markets outside of Virginia. A number of warehouses were constructed in Petersburg to manage the traffic, and inspectors graded the tobacco as it reached the structures. These warehouses were strictly controlled by laws of the General Assembly, and the governor appointed the inspectors.

After acquiring his land, William Boisseau began construction of a residence, which he named Tudor Hall, and it was completed by 1812. Tudor Hall was located on high ground near a stream known as Arthur's Swamp. The house faced north toward a road known as "Lew Jones Road" and "Courthouse Road" and which later became the Petersburg and Boydton Plank Road. At an as yet unknown date, a farm lane called Duncan's (later Duncan) Road was built through the Boisseau property to the east of Tudor Hall. This road was probably constructed in stages and eventually connected surrounding farms to the Squirrel Level and Vaughan roads south of the house. All of these roads were used to roll the large hogsheads of tobacco from the fields to the warehouses in Petersburg.

The house was made of pine and was a two-and-a-half story, four-bay, wood-frame residence constructed on a raised brick basement. This two-room, hall-and-parlor plan was a traditional form popular in Dinwiddie County during the latter part of the 1700s and the early part of the 1800s. Brick chimneys were constructed on the east and west gable ends of the house. Tudor Hall was representative of houses built in the county by upper-middle to middle-upper income farmers. In the late 1700s, a residence like Tudor Hall would probably have been owned by a household in the upper five percent of the population. Dinwiddie farmers preferred to spend their money on slaves, land, or stocks and bonds rather than on large and expensive homes. Tudor Hall exhibited both Georgian- and Federal-style characteristics in its exterior and interior. The origin of the name Tudor Hall is not known. It first appears in legal documents when a part of the farm was transferred to one of William's sons in 1839.

A number of outbuildings were eventually erected around Tudor Hall, but the lack of early source materials does not allow for speculation on precisely what they were or when they would have been built. These structures likely would have included a kitchen, smoke house, privy, corn crib, ice house, well house, carriage shed, and slave quarters. The farm would also have included livestock sheds and buildings for storing farm implements. From Tudor Hall, the

Tudor Hall in the 1920s

COURTESY MRS. MARY MARGARET WOOD

Boisseaus could see their tobacco fields on all sides. Wooded areas along the ravines and wetlands areas of Arthur's Swamp might have been used both to graze livestock and for timbering.

William Boisseau, who was born in the 1780s, had married Athaliah Keziah Wright Goodwyn in 1808. The Boisseaus eventually had seven children who survived to maturity--William E., Jr., Martha Eliza T., Albert Winfield, Joseph Goodwyn, Leander L., Andrew J., and Ann E. Tax rolls for 1815 show that William Boisseau owned 14 slaves. According to the 1820 census, he owned 25 slaves. He had increased that number to 40 by the time of the 1830 census. The 1820 census showed that William Boisseau was in business with David Boisseau, who probably was an older brother. David's home was east of the Boydton Plank Road just north of Hatcher's Run. That census also indicated that William was a tobacco inspector. Six people in William's household worked as agriculturalists.

Beginning in 1820, William Boisseau purchased a number of other land parcels, and he owned approximately 990 acres by the end of the decade. Because the cultivation of tobacco exhausted the soil, farmers had to acquire as much acreage as possible. The crop would be planted on different fields to slow the rate of soil exhaustion, and Boisseau would have grown some oats and wheat to try to revitalize worn-out fields. He also grew corn, which with the oats could be used as feed for his numerous farm animals. Under normal circumstances, the upland fields would produce profitably for no more than two to three years. Forest land would then be cleared for the tobacco. Farmers would either plant wheat and corn on the old fields or use them as pasture land for their animals. Some farmers let their exhausted fields remain fallow for a year or two before putting a crop on them again.

From 1830 until his death, William Boisseau prospered at Tudor Hall. His farm represented a largely self-supporting, self-contained economy and lifestyle. Surviving tax records indicate that his personal wealth grew during the 1830s. In addition to his duties as a farmer, Boisseau worked as an inspector at Moore's Warehouse in Petersburg. As previously mentioned, he had held this or a similar position since at least 1820. Dinwiddie County records show that he posted a $4,000 bond when appointed by the governor each year from 1834 to 1838. Tobacco inspectors occupied an important place in Dinwiddie and Petersburg society. That Boisseau was respected by his neighbors and peers is shown in his obituary, which appeared in the <u>American Constitution</u>: "He died as he lived, an honest man, the noblest work of God."

William Boisseau's continued prosperity was at odds with the general trend in much of Virginia at that time. During the years 1820-1840, the state experienced a decline in both white and slave populations. Farmers were moving to newer, more fertile lands in Kentucky, Tennessee, and the Deep South because of the exhaustion of the tobacco fields. It was cheaper for them to do this than to buy the additional slaves needed to try to restore the land. Accordingly, slaves were being sold by Virginians to planters in the Deep South, particularly the states of Georgia, Alabama, and Mississippi, where cotton agriculture required large numbers of field hands.

All of William and Athaliah's children had been born by 1830. William, Jr., married in 1837 and left home. He received from his father 128 acres of land on Arthur's Swamp and six slaves. Martha Eliza T. Boisseau married Robert H. Jones in 1834. Her father gave her seven slaves after her marriage. She died on February 29, 1840, and was buried in the family cemetery. This burial ground was located behind Tudor Hall and was surrounded by a wall of granite blocks. A survey of the property by the Works Progress Administration in 1936 stated that Martha's grave was a small square vault with a marble top. This stone, which can now be seen in Blandford Cemetery, was carved by Mountjoy and Lyon of Richmond. The inscription reads, in part, that the stone was "affectionately erected as a memorial of A Husband & Fathers love." Because the stone states that two infant children were buried with Martha, she may have died giving birth to twins who did not survive.

On November 22, 1838, William Boisseau died. An inventory of his property was made the following June. This inventory included his holdings on all six parcels of the land he owned and only the listing of household items can be tied to Tudor Hall. The inventory showed that he owned 51 slaves--18 males, 16 females, and 17 children. The estate included 9 horses, 55 cattle, 15 sheep, 60 hogs, and 300 fowl (turkeys, chickens, ducks, and geese). Farm products totaled 3,000 pounds of bacon, beef, and lard; 200 barrels of corn; 20,000 pounds of fodder and sheave oats; and 12,000 pounds of tobacco. Boisseau owned one carriage and harness, two wagons and gear, and two ox carts. He also owned two "Farm Mills" with two grinding stones. These mills may have been located on Arthur's Swamp, as tax records show buildings on that parcel.

Athaliah Boisseau inherited her husband's property after his death. In 1839, she regained the land given her son William, Jr., who had moved to Alabama. Her holdings increased again in 1840, when she inherited nearly 520 acres on Reedy Branch. The following year, Athaliah deeded 300 acres on Reedy Branch east of Tudor Hall to her son Albert W. and 396 acres on Great Creek to her son Joseph. The 1840 census listed Athaliah as the head of the household at Tudor Hall. She owned 14 male and 21 female slaves. In addition to her children, there were several others living in the household with Athaliah. These probably were her son-in-law Robert H. Jones and his two young sons. Eighteen of the people living in Tudor Hall were engaged in agriculture. The farm had been a successful enterprise for the Boisseau family during its first thirty years. That success would continue, though the nature of the farm would change in the next two decades.

CHAPTER 2

ANTEBELLUM ENTREPRENEURS

In Virginia during the 1820s and 1830s, there was, as stated, a trend of declining populations of whites and blacks. This trend continued in the 1840s. Travelers through the Tidewater and Piedmont reported seeing lands completely exhausted by tobacco farming. Small farmers continued moving into the Deep South. In addition to the slaves sold to the cotton states of the Gulf Coast, the number of slaves in Virginia was reduced by manumission. Slave owners voluntarily freed their chattels as a part of their wills. This situation began to change in the 1850s, however. Men like Prince George County planter Edmund Ruffin were challenging their neighbors to change their exploitive practices and to use various fertilizers. Gypsum, marl, and guano (especially that imported from Central and South America) helped revitalize the soil. Farmers also began to use nitrogen-fixing plants such as the Southern cow pea, and they adopted improved four or five-crop rotations, in which wheat and clover alternated with the traditional corn and tobacco fields. The advent of new technology--such as soil analysis and more sophisticated plows and implements--also decreased the need for a larger labor force. This resulted in a further reduction in the number of slaves in the state. Agricultural societies were formed and pushed the reforms urged by Ruffin and others in publications such as DeBow's Review and Southern Planter.

Internal improvements bolstered the reviving agricultural economy. Petersburg became the focal point for several railroad lines. The first to be completed was the Petersburg and Weldon Railroad in 1833. This line made Petersburg a market for farm produce from the Carolinas. The Richmond and Petersburg Railroad was completed by 1838 and permitted the shipment of wheat from Dinwiddie County to mills in the capital city. The Virginia General Assembly incorporated the South Side Railroad in 1846. It was to parallel Cox Road, which ran westward from Petersburg just south of the Appomattox River. In 1854, the South Side was complete between Lynchburg and the Battersea Cotton Factory. That same year, the railroad's owners bought the Appomattox Railroad, which connected Petersburg and City Point. By 1858, the Norfolk and Petersburg Railroad was completed. In 1850, the General Assembly chartered the Petersburg and Boydton Plank Road. The company corduroyed with logs the old Courthouse Road near Tudor Hall, making it easier for wagons to travel into Petersburg from the Dinwiddie countryside. The Board of Directors of the road had problems keeping up the road because the logs frequently became rotten.

Joseph G. Boisseau began running the Tudor Hall farm during the late 1840s. By 1850, Athaliah had moved from the house to live with her son-in-law Robert H. Jones on nearby Church Road. Between 1851 and 1857, Joseph undertook a major renovation to the house. This included a one-bay addition on the east end of the structure, extending and enlarging the east room. The original end wall was removed, and a new partition wall was constructed to create a center hall. The interior woodwork in the center hall and the rooms on the east side of the center hall on both the first and second floors was refurbished in the Greek Revival style. Other Greek Revival modifications were made, including a handsome staircase in the center hall. On the exterior, Greek Revival-style entrance porches were constructed on the front and rear elevations of the house. It is possible that the kitchen was moved from a separate building to the basement of the house at this time and a wood dining room floor was installed. Iron stoves were readily available during the 1850s from iron foundries in Petersburg and Richmond, and quickly became popular because of their convenience and the reduced chance of fire. The assessed value of the buildings on the farm more than doubled after Joseph remodeled Tudor Hall. This change may not be entirely accounted for by the remodeling; additional outbuildings may also have been constructed.

As stated, Athaliah Boisseau had moved out of Tudor Hall by 1850. The Federal census for that year showed her living with Robert H. Jones, Sr., in his home on nearby Church Road. He had married Athaliah's other daughter, Anne E., after the death of his first wife, Martha. Joseph Boisseau and Ann Jane Clarke, daughter of Thomas E. Clarke and Ann Jackson Clarke, were married at 8 p. m. on November 15, 1842, by Reverend Joseph W. Roper of the Methodist-Episcopal Church. Joseph and Ann had several children, but none of them lived to maturity. Surviving records for Dinwiddie County show that the Boisseaus had two daughters--Etta Ann, born September 17, 1851, and Josephine G., born August 30, 1853--and a son, Thomas Clarke, born on June 17, 1855. Josephine died on April 15, 1854; Etta Ann on October 18, 1859; and Thomas on April 30, 1860. The births of three children in the 1850s helps explain Joseph's renovation and expansion of Tudor Hall during that decade.

The sale of 35 acres to John W. Harmon in 1858 and of 20 acres to Charles Carr in 1859 reduced the size of the Tudor Hall tract to almost 240 acres. On January 5, 1861, Joseph finally bought the property from his mother for $1,400. The deed stated that "it is expressly understood that the grave yard on said land is mine [Athaliah's] and to remain unmolested." Inaccurate land records resulted in the deed reading that Joseph purchased only 175 acres.

COURTESY MRS. MARY MARGARET WOOD

Tudor Hall in the 1930s

Joseph Boisseau was a respected and apparently prominent member of the community in northern Dinwiddie County during the 1840s and 1850s. Surviving records indicate that he took an active role in several facets of official life in the county. On several occasions, he was appointed with other prominent citizens as "viewers" to investigate proposed road construction or changes in roads. These men reported back to the County Court on whether or not this road work would create any inconveniences to the public and if it would result in the destruction of any yards, gardens, or orchards. In late December 1859, Joseph was named as one of "three discreet and disinterested free holders" who were to examine the Boydton Plank Road in the middle of the next month. A complaint had been made that the company was not keeping the road repaired. The three men met at the one-mile post and found that the road indeed "was out of repair according to the true interest and meaning of the acts" of the General Assembly.

All of the roads in Dinwiddie County, most of them made only of dirt, needed occasional maintenance to make sure that crops could be taken to market without a great deal of trouble. To take care of the roads, the County Court appointed men as "surveyors." Each surveyor was responsible for using his own slaves and those of neighboring plantations and farms to carry out needed repairs. Joseph Boisseau's hands worked both on the Boydton Plank Road and Duncan Road during the 1850s.

Joseph Boisseau occasionally served on grand juries and petit juries and was on at least one coroner's jury during this time period. He was paid from 50 cents to $1.00 for these duties. The County Court also appointed him to help appraise the estates of persons who had died. Joseph Boisseau received appointments a number of times as an election commissioner in the county's Seventh District. In November 1859, he was appointed a member of Captain Winston Sutherland's company, which was to patrol District 7. This came in response to John Brown's raid on Harper's Ferry, which heightened fear of slave insurrections and other invasions of the state by abolitionists.

Since the agricultural schedule of the 1850 census listed the Tudor Hall property under the name "Joseph G. Boisseau per Andrew," it is possible that the brothers were both farming the property. Seventy-five acres of land were improved (under cultivation), and 185 acres were left unimproved. The unimproved land was probably forested or swamp land. The cash value of the farm was $2,500. The value of the farm implements and machinery was $125. Livestock on the farm included three horses, seven dairy cows, six other cattle, one working ox, and 50 hogs. Farm products included Indian corn, oats, peas and beans, Irish potatoes, and sweet potatoes. Additional products included butter, hay, and beeswax and honey. According to the 1850 slave schedules, Joseph Boisseau owned only eight slaves--six females and two males (one of them a child).

The 1860 census indicates that the previous decade had been a prosperous one for Joseph Boisseau. His real estate was valued at $5,500 and his personal estate was worth $402. He owned 18 slaves--11 males and seven females. One of the female slaves was a fugitive from the state. There were 119 improved acres and 100 acres of unimproved land on the farm. The value of the farm implements and machinery was $1,040. Livestock included two horses, two mules, four dairy cows, 11 other cattle, and 14 hogs. Joseph's farm products included wheat, Indian corn, oats, peas and beans, Irish potatoes, and sweet potatoes. Other farm products included 10 gallons of wine and 200 pounds of butter.

A comparison of census and tax data from 1850 to 1860 reveals several interesting changes which correspond to general trends of diversification affecting the type and size of farming operations during that decade. The ratio of improved to unimproved land changed, indicating either new or restored cultivated fields at work. Noting that by 1860 Joseph had added a wheat crop, increased his production of oats by 25 percent, and reported the production of hay for the first time, these changes parallel the shift to diversification reported by his contemporaries in the widely-read agricultural journals. Joseph was also using peas and beans, which were "manuring" crops that replenished soil nutrients as well as capacity to be sold at market. The introduction of wheat cannot be entirely attributed to its role as a staple in the plantation economy. By 1860, Richmond's stature as a milling export center was exceeded only by Baltimore, and its proximity to Petersburg commission houses provided a tremendous opportunity for profit and a ready market for all the wheat that could be purchased. The location of the Boydton Plank Road close to Tudor Hall probably bolstered the value of Joseph's crops and lands, as well as making easier the shipment of produce to Petersburg.

Between the years 1850-1860, the value of the farm more than doubled. The renovation of Tudor Hall and the improvement of the Boydton Plank Road undoubtedly contributed to this rise but were not the primary factors in the increase. More importantly, the improvement of farm land and crops were responsible for the change. Another indication that land improvement significantly contributed to this appreciation is the approximately 832 percent increase in the value of farm implements, from $125 in 1850 to $1,040 in 1860. In spite of the fact that the numbers and types of livestock remained fairly stable between 1850 and 1860, their value increased, perhaps due to an investment in improved breeds of hogs and cattle. Although Joseph Boisseau is listed as owning 8 slaves in 1850, with an increase to 18 in 1860, the overall numbers of slaves at Tudor Hall had declined from his father's time. The decrease reflects the disappearance of tobacco on the farm, a crop which Joseph had discontinued as early as 1850. Money was being shifted from slaves to investments in agricultural machinery.

Thus, on the eve of the Civil War, Tudor Hall exemplified the "new" agriculture. As a planter oriented more toward diversification than the previous form of agriculture practiced by his father, Joseph Boisseau represented a newer breed of farmer--one whose stable economic base ultimately reduced the dominance of the old-style colonial plantation. His comfortable lifestyle was about to be forever changed, however. Sectional controversies that had flared off and on since the late 1840s would soon erupt in armed conflict between the Southern and Northern states.

CHAPTER 3

MILITARY HEADQUARTERS

Virginia seceded from the Union on April 17, 1861, after the bombardment of Fort Sumter in Charleston Harbor, South Carolina, and the call of President Abraham Lincoln for volunteers to supress the "rebellion." The state's ordnance of secession was put before the voters for their approval on May 23. Dinwiddie County's men overwhelming supported the break from the union--804 to 1. In the meantime, military companies began forming in the county, and eventually at least six companies were mustered into the army of the Confederate States of America. Joseph Boisseau was not among the men in those companies. He may have been either too old for military service or have had some kind of exemption. It is known that he rented slaves from his mother. By adding those to the slaves he owned outright, Joseph might well have qualified for an exemption from the draft under the infamous "Twenty Negro Law," a provision in the conscription act that allowed one white man on each plantation with twenty or more slaves to avoid military service.

During the Civil War, in July 1861 and again in December 1862, he was named to the county's police force. This body was to carry out an ordinance passed by the state's secession convention on May 1, 1861. Joseph continued to receive appointments as an election commissioner, and he continued to serve on jury duty. He also acted as one of several commissioners who were to take bids for the repair or rebuilding of bridges on Hatcher's Run and Old Town Creek. In July 1862, he was named surveyor of Duncan Road in place of his brother Andrew. It is unknown how long Joseph served in this capacity. Records show that he was paid as a road "overseer" in July 1869.

The government of Virginia in early 1863 began conscripting (drafting) free blacks and slaves for work on fortifications. Several times during 1863-1864, slave owners in Dinwiddie and other counties were called upon to furnish laborers for the Petersburg defenses. On none of these occasions did Joseph Boisseau's name appear on the list of slave owners required to provide slaves. This may have been because, as shown on personal property tax records, he only owned nine slaves in 1863. At three different times, he was appointed by the county to help appraise the slaves before they were turned over to Confederate authorities. This appraisal involved not only a statement of the value of the slaves but preparation of a detailed physical description of each.

Even though, as will be described, Joseph and Ann Boisseau moved out of Tudor Hall in October 1864, he remained somewhat active in county affairs. The presence of so many Confederate soldiers in northern Dinwiddie resulted in the confiscation of supplies and some destruction of fences and buildings. This damage had reached a point by December 19, 1864, that the County Court took official notice of it. In its session on that day, the court decided to appoint a commissioner who was to confer with Confederate authorities about what might be done to curtail the destruction.

FROM U. S. WAR DEPARTMENT, ATLAS TO ACCOMPANY THE OFFICIAL RECORDS OF THE UNION AND CONFEDERATE ARMIES (WASHINGTON, D. C.: GOVERNMENT PRINTING OFFICE, 1891-1895), PLATE XL-1

Detail from an 1863 Confederate Engineers Map - "Map of the Approaches to Petersburg and Their Defenses, 1863." Tudor Hall is at the bottom center. It is labeled "Boisseau."

Joseph Boisseau was named as that commissioner, but no record exists that describes his activities on behalf of the citizens of the county.

No significant documentary evidence survives to tell how Joseph and Ann Boisseau operated the Tudor Hall farm during the war years. Military maps drawn by Confederate and Union engineers in 1863 and 1867, respectively, and accounts written by soldiers stationed on the Tudor Hall tract provide some clues. The Confederate map indicates at least two clearly delineated fields under cultivation on the west side of Duncan Road. That area of the farm east of Duncan Road was composed of wood lots or fallow fields left to succession. The Union map shows the house, several out-buildings, and three farm structures on the west side of Duncan Road. The house and at least one outbuilding lay within a fenced precinct which also probably contained a kitchen garden, other ornamental plantings, and the family cemetery.

Even as late as the summer of 1864, crops were being sown and harvested in Dinwiddie County despite the shortages of seed, implements, and labor. Captain William S. Dunlop, commander of a Confederate sharpshooter battalion, wrote that corn was being planted, if not harvested, by its owner in the vicinity of Tudor Hall in August. Joseph Boisseau's brother Albert had planted one of his fields in sorghum that year, and it does not seem unreasonable to assume that Joseph also grew sorghum. An indication that Joseph was contuining to prosper during the war is the fact that in June 1863 he purchased ten acres of land on the Boydton Plank Road. He paid $500 for the property. Joseph did not own the land for long, however; he sold it to Armstead Poland in March 1864.

The war remained somewhat remote for the residents of northern Dinwiddie County during its first three years.

No enemy soldiers threatened the county and the City of
Petersburg until the summer of 1864. Union armies led by
Lieutenant General Ulysses S. Grant closed in on the Confederate capital then. Unable to defeat General Robert E.
Lee's Army of Northern Virginia in open battle, Grant decided to capture Petersburg. Many of the roads and rail-
roads that brought badly needed supplies into Richmond
passed through Petersburg. If the Federals could take the
city, Lee would be forced to abandon Richmond. The initial
Union attack in June failed, and Grant was forced to con-
duct siege operations. Over the next several months, his
men gradually stretched their entrenchments to the west,
cutting off several supply routes.

Following the Battle of Globe Tavern in late August 1864,
Grant's army permanently cut the Weldon Railroad at that
spot. Lee's army could still draw supplies from that rail-

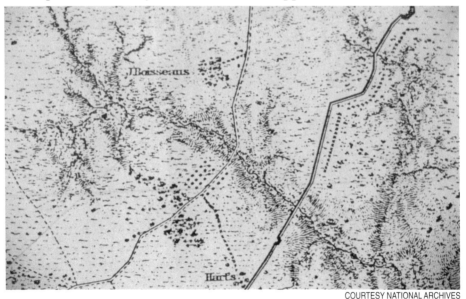

COURTESY NATIONAL ARCHIVES

Detail from "Map of Union Siege Works and Confederate Defenses around
City of Petersburg," by Major Nathaniel Michler, U. S. Engineers, 1867

road, however. Trains coming up from North Carolina could reach a station eighteen miles below Petersburg. From that point, supplies were transferred to wagons and taken to Dinwiddie Court House. Then the wagons traveled up the Boydton Plank Road into Petersburg. Lee's engineers began extending the army's trench lines westward from the city in mid-September 1864 to protect the Plank Road. The earthworks now preserved on Pamplin Park Civil War Site were part of this expansion.

Union troops attempted to reach and cut the Boydton road in late September. The Battle of Peebles's Farm (September 30-October 2) resulted in the defeat of this effort by the Federal army. Parts of this battle occurred east of Tudor Hall on the farm of Dr. Albert Boisseau, and shortly after the fighting, Union soldiers burned his house. The two armies skirmished along Duncan Road south of Tudor Hall near the Carr house on October 2. During the following months, Confederate troops of Major General Cadmus M. Wilcox's and Major General Henry Heth's divisions of Lieutenant General Ambrose P. Hill's Third Corps established camps in the area and worked to strengthen the line of fortifications, which ultimately stretched to Hatcher's Run. Brigadier General Samuel McGowan's brigade of Wilcox's division was stationed near Tudor Hall and built the entrenchments on the Boisseau farm. The brigade consisted of the 1st South Carolina (Provisional Army), 12th South Carolina, 13th South Carolina, 14th South Carolina, and Orr's South Carolina Rifles infantry regiments. McGowan soon moved into Tudor Hall, making it his brigade's headquarters.

The precise date that General McGowan took over Tudor Hall as his brigade headquarters is unknown, but it undoubtedly was in early October 1864 after the Battle of Peebles's Farm. Joseph and Ann Boisseau moved out of the

Brigadier General Samuel McGowan

house and may have moved into Petersburg, where other family members were living. McGowan, who was born in 1819, had been a lawyer before the war, had served in the South Carolina house of representatives, and had fought in the Mexican War. He had been a major general in the state militia from the time of South Carolina's secession until the Battle of First Manassas. There he was an aide-de-camp on the staff of Brigadier General Milledge Bonham. Later McGowan received an appointment as lieutenant colonel of the 14th South Carolina Infantry Regiment. He assumed command of the unit when its colonel resigned in April 1862.

McGowan served well in several battles and was wounded in the battles of Gaines's Mill and Sharpsburg. The death of Brigadier General Maxcy Gregg at Fredericksburg resulted in McGowan's promotion to command the brigade. At the Battle of Chancellorsville, McGowan suffered a severe wound in the leg. This injury kept him off duty until February 1864, and he had to use a cane when he returned to his brigade. After gallant service in the Battle of the Wilderness, McGowan was wounded a fourth time at Spotsylvania while leading his men in a counterattack at the Bloody Angle or Mule Shoe. He did not return to duty until August, by which time his brigade was involved in the Petersburg Campaign. McGowan continued to lead his men until the surrender at Appomattox Court House. After the war, he served in the South Carolina legislature and as an associate justice of the state supreme court. McGowan died in 1897.

When McGowan's staff moved into Tudor Hall, it consisted of the following officers: Captain Langdon Cheves Haskell, assistant adjutant general; Major Harry Hammond, brigade quartermaster; Captain Ralph E. B. Hewetson, assistant quartermaster; Captain Robert L. McCaughrin, assistant quartermaster; Major Andrew Bowie Wardlaw, brigade commissary; Captain John Gibson Edwards, assistant commissary; Second Lieutenant C. Gratiot Thompson, brigade ordnance officer; Dr. Thomas Alexander Evins, brigade surgeon; and Lieutenant James Fitz James Caldwell, aide-de-camp. Several changes in McGowan's staff occurred while the brigade was camped on the Boisseau farm. Captain Haskell transferred to the staff of Lieutenant General Richard H. Anderson and was replaced in early December by Captain James W. Riddick. In mid-November, Captain Edwards became assistant commissary on Wilcox's staff. Captain McCaughrin resigned later that month and early in 1865 was appointed first lieutenant and adjutant of the 14th South Carolina.

In addition to these staff officers, Tudor Hall would have been used by various captains and lieutenants from the brigade who were serving as officers of the day. Most of the staff officers would have had orderlies or clerks assisting them in keeping up with the mounds of paper on which the army seemed to float. Additionally, men on guard duty and personal servants would have moved in and out of Tudor Hall.

According to an account written after the war by Lieutenant Caldwell, the general and his staff enjoyed the time they spent at Tudor Hall. Caldwell remembered that McGowan frequently received visits from a number of other generals, including division commanders Henry Heth and Cadmus Wilcox and fellow brigade commanders like William MacRae. Caldwell wrote, "General McGowan was a hearty, genial, entertaining host; and he could get more fun into a game of whist than I had imagined it possible to inject into that serious recreation." The officers at Tudor Hall did not have many books to help them while away the time, so several of them would recite lines from various poems and plays. McGowan himself led recitals from some of his favorite authors, including William Shakespeare and Milton. The general taught Caldwell the lines to the popular poem "My Life is Like the Summer Rose," by Richard Henry Wilde.

A significant part of the Tudor Hall story during the Civil War revolves around Caldwell. He was born in Newberry, South Carolina, on September 19, 1837. Caldwell attended South Carolina College, studied law in Charleston, and was admitted to the bar in January 1859. He joined the 1st South Carolina Infantry in April 1862. After serving as military secretary to the regiment's commander, Caldwell was promoted to the rank of lieutenant and was assigned to Company B. In late 1862, McGowan, then colonel of the 14th South Carolina, began urging Caldwell to write a history of their brigade, which was commanded by Brigadier General Maxey Gregg. Caldwell did not feel qualified for the task and demurred. After being wounded in August 1864, Caldwell rejoined the brigade in the middle of November and was appointed to be McGowan's aide-de-camp. This left the lieutenant with, as he put it, "no excuse...for not writing the brigade history."

Caldwell was pleased to learn that he did not have to perform any of the routine duties expected of a staff officer. The general promised to give him any assistance needed. McGowan even turned over to Caldwell use of his room in Tudor Hall. While there, Caldwell had access to all of the brigade's official reports and correspondence, as well as some records of the division to which the brigade was attached. He often spoke with the various regimental officers to obtain additional information. By late March 1865, Caldwell had finished about three quarters of the history. He began working on the manuscript again after he returned home at the end of the war. The History of a Brigade of South Carolinians: Known First as "Gregg's," and Subsequently as "McGowan's Brigade" was published by King and Baird,

Printers, of 607 Sansom Street, Philadelphia, in 1866. Caldwell's book is widely accepted as one of the finest Confederate unit histories and is unusual in that most of it was written during the war.

McGowan's men worked hard that winter in strengthening their line of earthworks and extending it toward the southwest. Caldwell recalled that duty:

...For nearly two months, a detail, varying from two hundred to three hundred and fifty men, was constantly at work here, except on Sunday, from eight o'clock A. M., to four P. M. These works were constructed according to rule--with a ditch in front of six feet depth and eight feet width, whence all the earth for the embankment was thrown; with an embankment of six feet height, twelve feet base, and four feet terreplein; with a strong, neat revetment, and a banquette tread. These works would conceal troops marching behind them, would afford perfect protection from small arms and ordinary field artillery fire, and they could scarcely be stormed, on account of the ditch and the brush abatis in front. This was hard work; for we had to walk at least two miles over ground almost always either shoe-deep in mud or frozen hard and rough, and we had to dig up earth frequently frozen to the depth of a foot, and at other times running streams of water....Each man's turn came every third or fourth day, for this work.

In addition to the main line of fortifications, the South Carolinians constructed a picket line. Caldwell described the latter: "The picket line ran about parallel with our works, and on an average of five hundred yards from them. In some places, this line had regular entrenchments, but, as a rule, we had only strong rifle pits. The pits were about ten paces apart."

Behind the trenches and around the Boisseau house, McGowan's troops pitched tents and built log huts to serve as their winter quarters. Archaeological excavations have revealed that these structures were close to the earthworks. This proximity to the fortifications made some soldiers nervous. Private Samuel L. Dorroh of the 14th South Carolina wrote his mother:

> ...We have just built our quarters on the line right in front of the yanks. We can see their line from our tent. Their breast works is about a mile off. Only a 1/2 to the skirmish line. We can hear their drums & horns very plainly. I fear they will take a notion & shell our camp some of these days....

These camps, the associated open space for drill and parade grounds, and supply and functional areas (such as messes and supply tents) probably covered the majority of acreage between Duncan Road and the line of earthworks, as well as the ground around Tudor Hall. The feet of hundreds of soldiers and dozens of animals slowly churned up the farm's fields, turning them into seas of mud or dust (when there was no rain).

The South Carolinians cut down much of the forest they found on the Boisseau farm during the winter. They used the trees in the construction of the earthworks and huts and for firewood. Lee had ordered that his soldiers cut no timber in the rear of their entrenchments, so the men left some trees standing both for shade and perhaps to mask their movements from the enemy. One of McGowan's staff officers wrote that the troops cut mainly "green pine or swamp wood." Toward the end of the brigade's sojourn on the Tudor Hall property, wood had to be hauled by wagon from a mile or more away from the camps.

Some of the farm's outbuildings undoubtedly fell prey to the unceasing need for wood, but many of the structures apparently were not harmed. On December 29, 1864, Captain Riddick reported that, in the previous ten days, he had inspected the grounds upon which McGowan's Brigade were encamped. He stated that there had been no camps on the Boisseau farm prior to the brigade's occupation of the property and that he had "found the buildings out houses &c in a good state of preservation." Riddick went on to say, "No damages of any nature have been committed so far as I have been able to ascertain other than the destruction of forest trees for fuel, building of quarters &c." Although no assessment of the damages had been made, "the arrangements have been made for the prompt assessment under existing regulations." In late February 1865, Captain Riddick conducted another inspection of the grounds of Tudor Hall. He reported again that he "found the dwelling and out houses thereon in a good state of preservation." As he had claimed two months before, Riddick said, "No wanton damage have [*sic*] been committed and no damages of any nature, other than the destruction of trees &c for fuel & building of quarters." The captain was trying to arrange an assessment of the damages so that the Boisseaus could be compensated, but no evidence survives to show whether or not this was ever done.

Although the war was not going well for the Confederacy by early February 1865, the men of McGowan's Brigade adopted resolutions expressing their determination to continue fighting for as long as possible. Lieutenant Caldwell recalled that this document bore "as warlike a tone as the most ultra-secessionist could demand." Major Wardlaw, McGowan's commissary officer, wrote to his wife that the general himself had drawn up the resolutions. The latter were forwarded to the Confederate Congress, which had them published as flyers for general distribution. On the night after the meetings were held, the men of the brigade and their band conducted a torchlight parade from their quarters to Tudor Hall and asked McGowan to give a speech. He talked for about an hour, his address said to have been "abounding in fun & anecdotes."

Five months of relative quiet at Tudor Hall ended in March. McGowan's men lost their advance rifle pits to Union soldiers on the twenty-fifth. In response to a Confederate attack on Union Fort Stedman east of Petersburg, Major General George G. Meade ordered Major General Horatio G. Wright to send forward elements of his VI Army Corps, which was stationed on McGowan's front. The Federals advanced that afternoon against both McGowan's skirmish line and that of Brigadier General James H. Lane's brigade on McGowan's left. After brief but fierce fighting, the Confederates had to abandon their advance positions and establish a new line closer to the entrenchments. Another result of this skirmish was the destruction of the house of Robert H. Jones, Sr., which was located between the two armies's entrenchments. Confederate sharpshooters had fired on Union troops from its windows, so men of the 2nd Vermont Infantry Regiment burned the structure.

Late on March 29, most of McGowan's brigade left the fortifications near Tudor Hall and moved toward Hatcher's Run, where Lee was expecting an attack by elements of Grant's army. Four regiments of Lane's brigade replaced the South Carolinians except on the skirmish line, where McGowan's sharpshooters remained in the rifle pits constructed after March 25. Lane's brigade consisted of the 18th North Carolina, 28th North Carolina, 33rd North Carolina, and 37th North Carolina infantry regiments. Lane reported later that there were "from six to ten paces" between his men. The trenches on the Boisseau farm were held by members of the 37th North Carolina and a section (two cannon) of the Norfolk Light Artillery Blues.

Major General Horatio G. Wright   COURTESY NATIONAL ARCHIVES

Union forces attacked and defeated the Confederates on April 1 in the Battle of Five Forks. This victory opened the way toward the South Side Rail Road. Grant sensed that the initiative was clearly in his favor. He ordered Major General George G. Meade to make "a general assault along the lines" on the morning of April 2. Meade directed these orders to Wright and Major General John G. Parke, whose VI and IX Corps troops were concentrated directly in front of the proposed breakthrough areas. Meade instructed Parke and Wright to "attack at 4 a. m. the next day."

Wright followed up these orders by instructing his artillery to open fire immediately on the Confederate lines. This sparked a three-hour artillery duel that lit the skies from the Appomattox River to Union Fort Gregg. Wright's attack was planned to begin at precisely 4:00 a. m. on the morning of April 2. Realizing that it would be impossible to launch a coordinated attack until some sign of daylight appeared, Wright took it upon himself to postpone the assault for 40 minutes. At 4:40 a. m., Wright ordered the signal gun inside Fort Fisher to fire, which signaled the seventeen thousand Union troops, with fixed bayonets and uncapped muskets, forward across the open ground to their front.

By 5 a. m., troops of the VI Corps had broken through the Confederate defenses and had either captured its defenders or scattered them in disorder. A few men in gray fought briefly in McGowan's winter quarters but had to retreat toward Petersburg. The outer defenses of that city had been breached, and all supply routes into it had been cut. That night Robert E. Lee ordered the evacuation of both Richmond and Petersburg. Thus, the fighting that occurred at the Boisseau farm was a critical moment in the American Civil War. When Horatio Wright's men broke through the lines held by the troops of James Lane, the fate of the two cities was sealed.

CHAPTER 4

FROM MIDDLE CLASS
FARM TO HISTORIC SITE

Within a week of the Union army's breakthrough of the Confederate entrenchments near Tudor Hall, General Robert E. Lee surrendered the Army of Northern Virginia to Lieutenant General Ulysses S. Grant at Appomattox Court House. Four years of war had rendered such change to the South's agrarian economy and physical landscape that the traditional agricultural patterns and culture were not to be resurrected in its previous forms, especially considering the loss of personal property, land, and the labor force of black slaves. According to historian Virginius Dabney, in Virginia the wheat crop of 1865 "was an almost total failure," and the 1866 crop was "a partial failure." Outbuildings on farms and plantations had been dismantled for their lumber by troops from both armies. Wooden fences that bounded fields containing either crops or livestock were used as firewood or in the construction of field fortifications or winter quarters. Livestock, stored foods and meats, and even personal articles were appropriated by the soldiers.

Military occupation and the fighting that occurred around Tudor Hall left the farm devastated. Joseph and Ann Boisseau probably returned to their home shortly after the armies left the area. When the Tudor Hall tract was deeded to a trustee in 1868, some personal property was in the house and on the property: "household and Kitchen furniture, including bed & bedding Silver ware of every description; one gold watch, one two horse carriage, two mules and one horse, one buggy, [and] all of his farming utensils of every description." It is unknown whether or not Joseph made attempts to plant any crops on the land after the war ended. His slaves had been freed and likely did not return to the farm. By 1870, trees had again begun growing on the fields that had once produced tobacco, wheat, oats, and corn.

After Joseph and Ann Boisseau returned to Tudor Hall at the end of the Civil War, he resumed his role in county activities. He again served as an election commissioner and on grand jury duty. The emancipation of the slaves as a result of the war created in the white community tensions concerning the economic status of the new freedmen. In November 1865, the county appointed police forces of ten men each in every magisterial district. Joseph Boisseau became captain of the District 7 force and served in that capacity until at least June 1868. His pay ranged from $8.00 in 1866 to $15.20 in 1868. The County Court's appointment order also described the responsibilities of this law enforcement body:

> The duties of this police shall be to cooperate with the military and the other civil authorities in the prevention of crime and the maintenance of law, and order. They are hereby authorized and instructed to arrest all persons whom they directed by the warrant of a Justice to arrest or whom they have cause to suspect have violated the law or intend so to do; and all persons know[n] in law as vagrants--such persons as are going about without any employment or visible means of support; but they will not interfere with such as are honestly and in good faith seek-

ing employment. All Freedmen and Free Negroes arrested by them will be delivered to the officers of the Freedmen Bureau and all white Persons so arrested turned over to a Justice of the Peace to be dealt with according to law. They will also cooperate with the Freedmens Bureau under instruction from the Superintendent of the Freedmen. The authority of this police is confined to the County, but any policeman may act as such in any part of the County and require the assistance of any policeman or citizen as Sheriffs are authorized by law to do. They are authorized to use whatever force is necessary but not to kill an offender except in defense of themselves. In the discharge of their duties they should exercise a fair discresion [sic] remembering that they are officers of the law and their object the good of society.

In February 1868, Joseph deeded the property to his brother-in-law, Fayette D. Clarke, as trustee. He may have done this because of advancing age (he was then about 50), bad health, or failure to make a living. The land was to be held in trust for Ann Jane Boisseau "to make sale of the property conveyed or any part thereof so conveyed by said Deed and to invest the proceeds there of in other property." Ann obviously became dissatisfied with Clarke as a trustee, because in June 1869 she revoked his power as such and appointed her husband as trustee in his place. On June 22, Joseph, as trustee and husband, and Ann sold the Tudor Hall tract (except the family cemetery) to Asahel H. Gerow of Orange County, New York, for $3,950. The 1870 census showed the Boisseaus as living in a hotel in Petersburg. In September 1877, they purchased from Annie M. Ferris 200 acres and a house named Delkeith on Cox Road, four miles from Petersburg. The Boisseaus were still living there when Joseph died on May 9, 1879.

Asahel H. Gerow   COURTESY MRS. MARY MARGARET WOOD

Mary T. Gerow

Many of the large plantations and farms in Virginia were broken up into smaller parcels after the Civil War. State officials tried to attract emigrants from the northern states to move to Virginia and establish farms. Individuals and families from states like New York, New Jersey, and Pennsylvania began finding homes in Dinwiddie and surrounding counties. One such case was that of Asahel H. Gerow, a farmer from Newburgh, in Orange County, New York. Gerow suffered from a heart condition and traveled to Petersburg in search of a new home. He thought that the warmer climate might improve his health. The fifty-one-year-old Gerow was, like the Boisseaus, a descendant of French Huguenots. In the 1680s, the Gerows (originally spelled Giraud) had arrived in New York. Asahel brought to Tudor Hall his wife, Mary Townsend Gerow, and their two youngest sons, Smith Townsend and Leonard Rogers. Two older sons remained in New York. Family tradition said that the Gerows also brought all their household goods to Tudor Hall and that those furnishings were still in the house in the 1970s.

Changes were made to Tudor Hall during the late 1800s and throughout the early to mid-1900s. Sometime in the late 1800s, the windows in the rooms on the west side of the hall were replaced. Most of the windows in the basement appear to have been replaced at the same time. It is possible that only the windows on the east side of the house were replaced during the 1851-1857 renovation, and that the original windows in the rooms on the west side of the house were left in place. Then, about 1870, when the Gerow family moved into the house after it had been vacant, they probably replaced the original windows due to decay and damage. The original partition wall between the two rooms of the basement was removed during the late 1900s, but the basement was still used as a dining-family room. Closets were installed in several spaces, and extensive repairs were made to the exterior. A small bathroom addition was added onto the back porch, necessitating widening of the porch deck and roof, removal of siding, and the installation of a new doorway. In 1953, a concrete floor was put in the basement. Other alterations about this time included replacing most of the exterior siding with new boards of comparable size and profile as the original beaded clapboards. Basement remodeling included the installation of a modern kitchen in the west room, new ceiling and floor finishes, and the installation of a motorized chair-lift.

The Tudor Hall tract remained in the Gerow family for the next three generations. In his will, Asahel Gerow appointed his son Smith T. Gerow executor of his estate, leaving all his personal property to his wife, Mary Townsend Gerow, and directing that upon her death all real estate be divided among their four sons. Asahel died March 28, 1887. Smith T. Gerow became the owner of Tudor Hall in March 1895 upon the death of his mother. In 1902, he and his wife, Margaret E. Gerow, purchased the remaining shared interest in the Tudor Hall tract from his three brothers and deeded the entire tract to his wife. Smith T. Gerow died November 8, 1930. Lilla Marie Gerow Diehl inherited Tudor Hall from her mother Margaret Estelle Bradt Gerow in August 1960. Mrs. Diehl received the portion of the property lying on the west side of Duncan Road (72 acres) including the house, and her brother Asahel Harmon Gerow received the portion lying on the east side of Duncan Road (102.9 acres). Lilla Gerow Diehl sold one acre of the property in 1967 and 2.66 acres in 1975. In 1994, the Co-Executors of the Estate of Lilla Gerow Diehl, Edward Townsend Diehl and Clark M. Wood, conveyed the remaining acreage of the Tudor Hall property, including the house, to the Pamplin Foundation.

When Asahel Gerow and his family moved into Tudor Hall, the farm was in no condition to be farmed without a complete restoration of agricultural fields, fences, and certainly some farm structures (such as livestock pens). Debris from the military occupation and fighting remained, erosion had affected the denuded landscape, and the earthworks posed a significant physical impediment by nearly severing the tract in two. With the combination of a degraded agricultural landscape and the weakened health of Asahel Gerow, the restoration of Tudor Hall to its prewar status seemed a formidable task. He engaged in farming and probably began the practice of allowing a black tenant to work the fields north of the house. Asahel's health did not improve, and he was said to have been an invalid when he died in 1887.

Smith T. Gerow took over operation of the farm, and he and his wife, Margaret Bradt Gerow, lived in Tudor Hall with his mother. He was responsible for the renewal of Tudor Hall as a farm landscape in the early 1900s. Between 1887 and 1930, Smith Gerow built numerous structures and relied upon tenant farmers, leased fields, and commercial timbering as the economic support for the farm in lieu of large-scale crop production. Most of the farm construction initiated by Gerow was limited to the vicinity near Tudor Hall house, where he built a new cluster of outbuildings between 1900-1930, including a barn, wellhouse with electric generator, privy, icehouse, corn crib, smokehouse, and lean-to woodshed next to the barn. Fences were rebuilt to keep out cows pastured near the house.

Only portions of the fields which were either planted or in pasture prior to the Civil War were returned to agriculture. The rest of the property was relegated to succession and forest restoration in order to support commercial timbering operations. On the eastern side of Duncan Road, there were two distinct crop fields in use throughout much of the 1900s, named the "front field" and "back field." The "front field" was originally farmed by tenants, and then it was leased to other area farmers until the early 1990s. The "back field" of 2.5 acres was Smith Gerow's "kitchen garden" and was later leased out to melon and cantaloupe farmers.

Timbering operations altered the landscape with the addition of access roads for hauling, cuts through the earthworks, and open areas for "saw mills" and loading operations. By 1937, there were at least two open sites within the wooded acreage west of Duncan Road, and three or four similar sites east of the road, all connected to Duncan Road by a web of dirt roads. At least one road ran along the south edge of the "front field" and was called "saw mill road." Wooded acreage in the eastern tract exhibited substantial areas of cut in 1937; however, approximately one-third to one-half of the timber appears not to have been cut over by that time. This is due to the fact that Smith Gerow would not allow timbering operations to affect the earthwork remnants before 1930. In other cases, such as land adjacent to Arthur's Swamp, timber cuts were made all the way down to the drainage, thus allowing for soil erosion on the sloped ravines similar to the situation present after the military occupation in 1864-1865. It appears that the scale of logging operations had diminished significantly by the 1950s-1960s, as timber now on the property represents approximately three decades of undisturbed growth.

One important alteration to the eastern wood lots occurred sometime around the turn of the century, when an easement for the Seaboard Railroad line was cut through the lower southeast corner of the property across the ravine and drainage to Arthur's Swamp. This railroad line was originally named the Richmond-Petersburg and Carolina Railroad in 1889 and was built to parallel the eastern seaboard along generally the same alignment as early American Indian trade routes. The railroad grade at Tudor Hall, built between 1917 and 1937, was still in operation in 1952;

however, it was abandoned after that. The trace alignment is still apparent on the Tudor Hall property.

In 1992, the Association for the Preservation of Civil War Sites (APCWS) became aware that timbering threatened some of the defensive fortifications on the Tudor Hall property. The need to preserve these valuable resources led APCWS to seek the support of the Pamplin Foundation of Portland, Oregon, in that effort. Because the leaders of that foundation are descendants of the Boisseau family, they entered into an agreement with APCWS to interpret and manage the land as Pamplin Park Civil War Site. More than 2,100 feet of earthworks, where the Union army broke through the Confederate lines on April 2, 1865, are preserved and protected. Upon the death of the owner of Tudor Hall in late 1994, the Pamplin Foundation purchased that structure and an additional 68 acres. The combination of the two parcels into a 171-acre site brought together the core of the historic Boisseau family farm on both sides of Duncan Road.

Tudor Hall has been restored to its appearance in 1864-1865. Today, the house reflects its dual occupancy during the Civil War years by Joseph and Ann Boisseau and later by Confederate officers. Rooms on the west side of the home are furnished as they might have looked in the spring of 1864 when the Boisseaus lived here. The rooms on the east side appear as they would have when used by the soldiers during the winter of 1864-1865. None of the furniture is original to the home, but all of it dates from the Civil War period. Exhibits in Tudor Hall's English basement tell briefly the history of the site and complete the interpretation of the house. The story of the Boisseau family and Tudor Hall is a tale repeated dozens of time across Virginia and the South during the first half of the nineteenth century. By studying that story, we can gain a greater understanding of and appreciation for the role of similar families and farms in the molding this nation.

APPENDIX

THE WILLIAM E. BOISSEAU FAMILY

William E. Boisseau (born 1780-1785; died November 22, 1838) married January 11, 1808, Athaliah Keziah Wright Goodwyn (born about 1793, daughter of Esau Goodwyn and Patsy Colson Tucker; died December 1864, Petersburg, Va.)

A. William E., Jr. (born 1809-1810; died January 3, 1854, Wetumpka, Ala.) married March 15, 1837, Julia B. Grigg (born 1817; died c. 1854, Wetumpka, Ala.)
1. Ella Athaliah (born December 20, 1845, or October 24, 1848, Wetumpka, Ala.; died February 20, 1924) married November 24, 1868 William James Beville
    a. Pauline (born November 1, 1874; died October 27, 1964) married January 27, 1898, John Robert Pamplin
2. Octavia (born 1846) married June 7, 1859, Edward Oscar Esau Pegram
3. William F. (born 1849)
4. Adrian P. (born 1848?)
5. Julia A. (born 1851) married November 16, 1869, Capt. W. L. Yager

   6. Martha Eliza (born 1853)

B. Albert Winfield (born 1814; died November 14, 1873) married Sarah A. ------
    1. Ann A. (born 1849)
    2. William (born 1852)
    3. George J. (born 1854)

C. Joseph Goodwyn (born February 27, 1817; died May 9, 1879) married November 15, 1842, Ann Jane Clarke (born June 18, 1828, daughter of Thomas E. Clarke and Ann Jackson; died after 1906)
    1. Etta Ann (born September 17, 1851; died October 28, 1859)
    2. Josephine G. (born August 2, 1853; died April 15, 1854)
    3. Thomas Clarke (born June 17, 1855; died April 30, 1860)

D. Martha Eliza T. (born July 21, 1819; died February 29, 1840) married May 21, 1834, Robert H. Jones
    1. William K. (born 1835)
    2. Robert H., Jr. (born 1838)
    3. two infants (died 1840?)

E. Leander L. (born 1822; died February ? 1859) married Mary R. ------

F. Ann E. (born 1825) married by 1850 Robert H. Jones

G. Andrew J. (born 1829?) married May 19, 1852, Susannah A. Goodwyn (daughter of Mary Goodwyn)
    1. James (born 1854)
    2. Charles F. (born 1856)
    3. Estelle (born 1858)
    4. four children by 1870

BIBLIOGRAPHY

"Boisseau Family." Tyler's Quarterly Historical and Genealogical Magazine, Vol. X (1928), pp. 118-30 and 280-83.

Caldwell, J. F. J. The History of a Brigade of South Carolinians. Philadelphia: King & Baird, 1866; reprint edition, Dayton, Ohio: Morningside Bookshop, 1992.

Caldwell, J. F. J. "Reminiscences of the War of Secession," in History of South Carolina. Ed. by Snowden Yates. Chicago, 1920. Vol. II.

Compiled Service Records of Confederate General and Staff Officers, and Nonregimental Enlisted Men, National Archives Microcopy No. 331.

Dabney, Virginius. Virginia: The New Dominion. Charlottesville: University Press of Virginia, 1971.

Diehl, Lilla Gerow "Tudor Hall and the Boisseau Family." Unpublished manuscript, 1980.

Dinwiddie County Court House: Works Progress Administration Records (Bible and cemetery records), Will Books, Deed Books, District Land Tax Books (1865-1889).

Dinwiddie County Court Minute Books, 1855-1869, Library of Virginia.

Dinwiddie County Register of Births, 1853, 1855, Library of Virginia.

"Dinwiddie County, Virginia, 1800 Tax List." Virginia Genealogist, XVIII (1974), p. 30.

Dorroh, Samuel Lewers, Papers, 1861-1868, Manuscript Division, South Caroliniana Library, University of South Carolina.

Dunlop, William S. Lee's Sharpshooters; or, The Forefront of Battle. Little Rock, Ark., 1899; reprint edition, Dayton, Ohio: Morningside Bookshop, 1988.

Fresles, W. Eugene, comp. Second Annual Directory for the City of Petersburg, To Which is Added a Business Directory for 1860. Petersburg, Va.: Published by George E. Ford, Bookseller and Publisher, 1860.

Jones, Richard L. Dinwiddie County: Carrefour of the Commonwealth. Richmond, Va.: Whittet & Shepperson, 1976.

Jordan, Ervin L. Black Confederates and Afro-Yankees in Civil War Virginia. Charlottesville: University Press of Virginia, 1995.

Petersburg The Daily Express, Oct. 29, 1859.

Petersburg Daily Post, May 10, 1879.

Petersburg Hustings Court Deed and Will Books.

Petersburg Index=Appeal, May 10, 1879.

Petersburg The Rural Messenger, May 17, 1879.

Scott, James G., and Edward A. Wyatt, IV. Petersburg's Story: A History. Richmond, Va.: Whittet & Shepperson, 1960.

Sommers, Richard J. Richmond Redeemed: The Siege at Petersburg. New York: Doubleday and Co., 1981.

U. S. Bureau of the Census. Population, Slave, and Agricultural Schedules for 1820, 1830, 1840, 1850, 1860, and 1870.

U. S. War Department. War of the Rebellion: Official Records of Union and Confederate Armies. 128 parts in 70 vols. Washington, D. C.: Government Printing Office, 1880-1901.

Wardlaw, Andrew Bowie, ed. Andrew Bowie Wardlaw of Abbeville and His Family. Charleston, S. C.: A. B. Wardlaw, 1989.

INDEX